this book belongs to

a Paul Doodles original

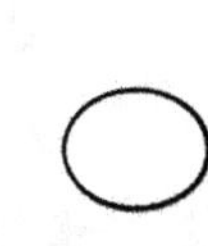

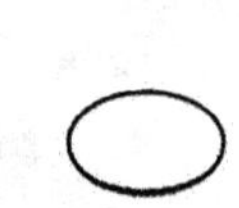

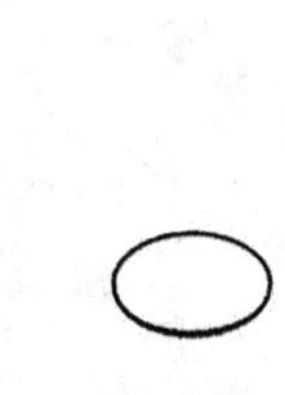

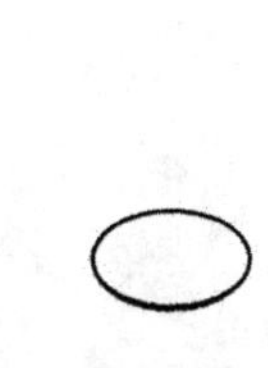

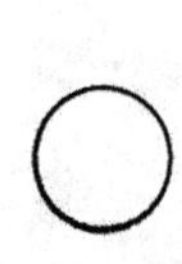

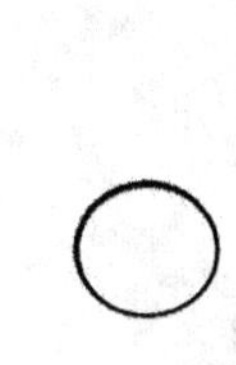

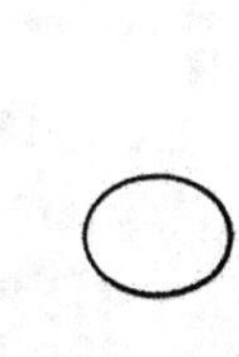

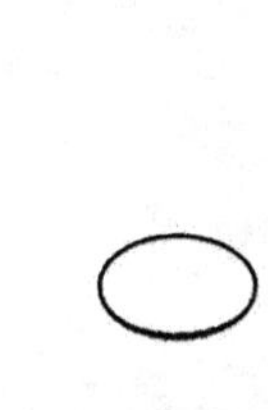

Time to get a new notebook